Participant Booklet

For the
Preparation Days
Retreat

This Book Belongs To:

Name_____

Phone _____

Address_____

Retreat Location _____

Retreat Time _____

Date _____

Participant Booklet

For the Preparation Days Retreat

By Ellen Tomaszewski

Published by Etcetera Press LLC

etcetera press

Richland, WA
Copyright 2013
ISBN: 978-1-936824-39-7

All rights reserved. No part of this book may be reproduced, stored in a retrieval system, or transmitted in any form or by any means, electronic, mechanical, photocopying, or otherwise, without written permission of Ellen Tomaszewski and Etcetera Press LLC.

Participant Booklet
For the
Preparation Days Retreat

Five Weeks of

Ignatian Prayer

Ellen Tomaszewski

Opening Prayer

Use this prayer to open each meeting.

1st Reader:

Jesus said, "Where two or three people come together in my name, I am there with you." Lord Jesus, here we are, gathered together in your name. So we ask you to help us see you today in this meeting.

2nd Reader:

Jesus, you also told us, "I am the light of the world… Whoever follows me will have the light of life and will never walk in darkness. (John 8: 12) We ask that you let the light of this candle symbolize your presence here among us, right now.

If permitted to do so in your facility, the person in charge of the prayer lights the candle.

3rd Reader:

Lord, Jesus, we believe that wherever you are, the Father and the Holy Spirit are there too. So we begin our meeting in your presence, and in the name of the Father, the Son, and the Holy Spirit. Amen.

Closing Prayer

Use this prayer to close each meeting.

1st Reader:

As we end our meeting, let's listen to the words Simeon spoke to Mary and Joseph in the temple about their child, Jesus.

2nd Reader:

"Now Master...my eyes have seen the salvation which you have prepared for all the nations to see, a light to enlighten the pagans and the glory of your people Israel." (Luke 2: 30-32)

Glory be to the Father, the Son, and the Holy Spirit.

Blow out the candle.

3rd Reader:

Lord, thank-you for your salvation, which enlightens the whole world. We know that even though we've blown out our candle, Christ's light continues to burn through and in each of us. Help us this week to let that light shine to others.

Now, together, let's pray the Lord's Prayer: "Our Father…"

Amen.

WEEK 1

Welcome to the Preparation Days Retreat!

This booklet will provide you with scriptures, prayers, and other materials for each week. We encourage you to spend time with the Lord every day, at least one-half hour, praying with the materials provided.

Today you begin a journey of discovery. But the journey is not outward. Instead, it will take you to the depths of your very soul.

Each meeting will consist of these parts.

1. We'll start with a prayer, introductions and a presentation on how to begin praying.
2. Your turn. You'll get the opportunity to pray.
3. Finally, you'll be able to talk to others about where God is in your life right now, and we'll close with a prayer.

For now, sit back, relax, and we'll tell you what to do next.

Question for Contemplating and Sharing:
Today you'll have time to pray individually before we go to our small groups. Use these questions.

- Where have I found God in the past week or so?
- Why am I here and what do I hope to gain?
- What if anything do I fear when I consider God or this retreat?

On the following lines, write what happened in your prayer time. This could be thoughts about the questions, feelings, ideas, revelations, or anything else.

Sharing

It's your turn to express yourself. So go to your assigned small group space. Read through the following instructions, then take turns talking about your prayer experiences, and listening to others in your group.

You will use the following instructions for your small group spiritual direction at every meeting.

Group Spiritual Direction Instructions

The purpose of Group Spiritual Direction is to keep our focus on what God is doing.

- Please don't solve other's problems
- Please don't give advice
- Keep the focus on the person who is sharing.

Speak
Each person in the group is invited to share his or her reflection. You don't have to share, but remember, this is how group spiritual direction works—people sharing their faith lives with others. It gives Spirit an opportunity to be active . As you share, address these questions:

- How did the reading affect me as I prayed?
- What was my experience?
- During my prayer, the strongest feeling I had was_____.
- Where was God in this experience for me?

Listen
Listeners are asked to focus on the speaker. Listen for God in what the person is sharing. What is God saying to that person? What is God saying to you as you listen? After a person has shared, the facilitator will invite you all to share your response to what you have <u>heard</u>.

- Share what you feel God is saying to that person.
- Share what you feel God is saying to you.

Review
At the end of the sharing session, once everyone has shared, take some time to evaluate the process.

- How well did we stay focused on each speaker?
- Any particular places where we went off-track (too much problem solving, too analytical, not attentive to the spirit?)
- How did each person feel about the meeting?

Method of Prayer
(5 Ps and C)

Use this method every day as you pray through the scriptures provided. Don't rush. Take your time with each step.

Place

Remember that God prays in us when we stop and let it happen. Of course listening to God requires a quiet place, a sacred space where you will be undisturbed for the time you pray. Choose a place where you can relax and be uninhibited in your response to God. Use the same place every day.

Passage

Mark your Bible the day before with the scripture for tomorrow so that it will be ready when you pray. You may also find it helpful to read the passage through a day ahead. This allows the scripture to unfold for you over time and for your subconscious to explore it.

Posture

The most important posture for prayer is one of quiet, both inside and out. Before you read any scripture, spend the first several minutes of every prayer time just relaxing your body. Don't rush. If this takes up the whole prayer time, that's okay.

- Quiet your mind.
- Breathe deeply and listen with intent to the sounds (or quiet) around you.
- Slowly sink yourself into the silence of your sacred space.

Presence

- Ask God's unselfish and loving presence to enter into you.
- Ask God for the grace to listen to what He has to say.

Pray

- Pray the passage from Scripture by reading it slowly aloud.
- Listen to the words. Really listen. Then read them again.
- Pause at words or phrases that speak to you or touch you in some way. Linger with those words. Think of them as precious gems. Cherish their beauty. Imagine God speaking them to you directly.

Close

- Finish your prayer with an Our Father since that is how Jesus taught us to pray.
- Write down what happened in your prayer – at least two sentences, more if possible. Explain insights, where God was or wasn't, how difficult or easy prayer was, and what you thought God was saying to you this day, as well as any strong desires that moved you.

Week 1, Day 1

John 10: 1-21—The Good Shepherd, Jesus, knows me

Pray with this scripture, following the five P's of Prayer. After your prayer time, please write your journal entry here. What did you feel, think, hope, discover about yourself, God, or the scripture?

_____

_____

_____

_____

_____

_____

_____

_____

_____

_____

_____

_____

_____

Week 1, Day 2

John 8: 1-12—Jesus doesn't condemn me, even for my worst sins. He is the light of the world.

Pray with this scripture. After your prayer time, please write your journal entry here. L:ke yesterday, write about your hopes, feelings, discoveries concerning God, prayer, self, or this scripture.

_____

_____

_____

_____

_____

_____

_____

_____

_____

_____

_____

_____

Week 1, Day 3

Mark 12: 1-12—Like the son of the vineyard owner who went to his vineyard, Jesus comes to me. How do I receive him?

Pray with the scripture using the 5 Ps. After your prayer time, please write your journal entry here.

Week 1, Day 4

Luke 5:27-32—Jesus said, "I have not come to call the virtuous, but sinners to repentance."

After your prayer time with the 5 Ps, please write your journal entry here.

Week 1, Day 5

Matthew 14: 13-21. Jesus feeds the hungry. When does Jesus feed me?

Pray this scripture, using the 5 Ps. Then write your journal entry here.

Week 1, Day 6

Mark 9:14-29—I do have faith, Lord. Help me when it falters.

Pray the scripture using the 5 Ps. Write your journal entry here.

Week 1, Day 7

Luke 15:1-32. I can understand more deeply about God's love through these parables.

I am precious , respected, and dear to God, who has been caring for me at every moment. After prayer, please write your journal entry here:

WEEK 2

Today's meeting focuses on the life of St. Ignatius and how it is relevant to the Spiritual Exercises. You will hear how Ignatius discovered the principles he used to develop these Exercises, as well as how he became a saint.

The meeting will consist of these aspects:
- Opening prayer (page 6)
- Presentation
- Personal prayer using questions in the next page
- Group spiritual direction
- Closing prayer (page 7)

Today's Questions for Personal Prayer And Small Group Spiritual Direction

- What attracts, repels, or surprises me about Ignatius' life?
- How does hearing about Ignatius affect me?
- How am I feeling at this moment about this retreat?
- What has God been telling me this past week? Is there a general theme that I can sort out or not?

Write your thoughts and feelings concerning your prayer here.

_____

_____

_____

_____

_____

_____

_____

_____

_____

_____

_____

At the end of this prayer time, go to your small group.
Use the instructions on the next page to share what you'd like.

Week 2
Group Spiritual Direction Instructions

The purpose of Group Spiritual Direction is to keep our focus on what God is doing.

- Please do not solve other's problems
- Please don't give advice
- **K**eep the focus on the person who is sharing.

Speak

Each person in the group is invited to share their reflection. You don't have to share if you do not want to, but, remember this is how group spiritual direction works. Sharing gives The Spirit an opportunity to be active within the group process.

- How did this reading affect you as you prayed?
- Share your experience.
- Share a feeling.
- Where was God in this experience?

Listen

Listeners are asked to focus on the person speaking. Listen for God in what the person is sharing. What is God saying to that person? What is God saying to you as you listen?

After a person has shared, the facilitator will invite you all to share your response to what you have heard.

- Share what you feel God is saying to that person.
- Share what you feel God is saying to you.

Review

At the end of the sharing session, once everyone has shared, take some time to evaluate the process.

- How well did we stay focused on each speaker?
- Any special places where we were off track (too much problem solving, too analytical, not attentive to the spirit)?
- How did each person feel about the meeting?

Instructions for This Week's Prayer

Your main job during this retreat is not finish this booklet, not "feel" God, but to discover the presence of God within yourself. Take your time. Don't rush through your prayer. Here's how.

Reflect on the fact that God sees you and rest in being beheld. You might tell God something like, "God, you know what I'm thinking and feeling. You know me. You, oh God, behold me right here, right now." Then sit with that thought for a while.

You can only do this if you let yourself slow down and relax. Don't rush. Take the time to appreciate God's care for you.

- Follow the 5 Ps & C (page 12 & 13) each day as you begin.
- At the end of your prayer, write in the pages provided what happened in your prayer.
- Spend time each day filling out each day's assignment in your Faith Autobiography booklet. Make sure the pages for this week are complete by the next group meeting.

Remember, these are *Exercises*, not a class. You can always repeat a scripture instead of moving to the next one. Don't worry about finishing the booklet, or about un-prayed scripture. That's not the point of the Exercises. The point is to grow closer to God.

We urge you to repeat any scripture that continues to speak to you. Do so until you feel it is "done."

Week 2, Day 1

Psalm 139 - God, you began my creation in my mother's womb, and continue to create me from nothing, for no reason other than love. Thank-you for the life you give me.

Pray with this scripture. Please write your journal entry here:

_____

_____

_____

_____

_____

_____

_____

_____

_____

_____

_____

_____

Week 2, Day 2

Luke 11:1-13 Lord, help me to learn to pray. Teach me.

Pray with this scripture. Then write your journal entry here:

Week 2, Day 3

Matthew 6:25-34 - Jesus tells us to consider how the lilies in the field depend on God.

God cares for me at every moment, in ways I can't imagine. I pray with this scripture. Then write my journal entry here:

_____

_____

_____

_____

_____

_____

_____

_____

_____

_____

_____

_____

Week 2, Day 4

Prayer of Consideration

(Based on a parable by Jesus)

Read this through slowly. Stop when you want to savor any part; take your time. If you don't finish it all, that's fine. You can use it again for as many days as it speaks to you.

Consider the lowly lily, growing in a field. It can't chose it's location. The soil might be rocky, sandy, dry, or wet, promoting growth or hindering it. There could be lots of rain, or little.

Like the lily, I'm in my own "field." I live in this century, in this country, city, neighborhood and family. A few of these I can change, like where I live, but I can't escape my time frame, my origin, or my genetics. I consider this a while.

The lily has no control over what grows around it. It might struggle to live with weeds or grazing animals. Or it might grow easily. I'm often like the lily, at the whim of my environment. Where is God in this?

A lily can't control wind, rain, or temperature; it just stands and takes whatever comes. In a way, I'm like that, too. I have little control over global issues such as wasted natural resources, war, climate change, or even simply, how others feel toward me. How does God fit into this?

The lily grows according to its genes. It's health depends on the climate, the soil, and what eats it. I became a certain person of a certain color and shape because of my genes, gotten from my parents. So much is influenced by what I've inherited, and where I live. How does God fit into this for me?

Jesus said that even Solomon dressed in fine clothing and jewels wasn't more lovely than the lily. And like the lily, I'm beautiful in God's eyes. Even though I sin, still God calls me beloved, and loves me as I am. How do I feel when I consider that God respects and cherishes me?

End with an *Our Father*.

After your prayer time, please write your journal entry on the next page.

Week 2, Day 5

Isaiah 43:1-7 - God wants me to know I am precious and loved.

I am redeemed by Jesus Christ who loves me and lives in me. After prayer, please write your journal entry here:

Week 2 Day 6

Psalm 139 again - God, thank you for creating my whole being.

God, Creator and Lord, continually creates me from nothing because God loves me passionately. How do I feel about this?

Pray with this scripture. After your prayer time, write here:

_____

_____

_____

_____

_____

_____

_____

_____

_____

_____

_____

Week 2, Day 7

Repeat Luke 11:1-13 Lord, teach me to pray. (Or use the following prayer):

Oh, Lord God, You knew me while I was in my mother's womb because you love me so much. You give me everything—movement, thoughts, dreams, hopes, and loves. You walk with me every moment of my existence. I am amazed that You pay attention to me and that You cherish me. Help me to trust you and remain faithful to you always. Amen.

After your prayer time, please write your journal entry here:

WEEK 3

Today's meeting focuses on meditation and how to begin praying with meditation. The meeting will have these sections:

- Opening prayer (page 6)
- Presentation
- Personal prayer using questions in the next page
- Group spiritual direction
- Closing prayer (page 7)

Questions for Prayer

- What did I experience when I realized it was Jesus speaking to me?
- How did I feel seeing the people who love me?
- What story that I told Jesus touched me the most? Why?
- Write your thoughts and feelings concerning your prayer here.

_____

_____

_____

_____

_____

_____

_____

_____

Group Spiritual Direction

The purpose of Group Spiritual Direction is to keep our focus on what God is doing.

- Please don't solve other's problems
- Please don't give advice
- Keep the focus on the person who is sharing.

Speak
Each person in the group is invited to share his or her reflection. You don't have to share, but remember, this is how group spiritual direction works—people sharing their faith lives with others. It gives Spirit an opportunity to be active . As you share, address these questions:

- How did the reading affect me as I prayed?
- What was my experience?
- During my prayer, the main feeling I had was _____.
- Where was God in this experience for me?

Listen
Listeners are asked to focus on the speaker. Listen for God in what the person is sharing. What is God saying to that person? What is God saying to you as you listen? After a person has shared, the facilitator will invite you all to share your response to what you have <u>heard</u>.

- Share what you feel God is saying to that person.
- Share what you feel God is saying to you.

Review
At the end of the sharing session, once everyone has shared, take some time to evaluate the process.
- How well did we stay focused on each speaker?
- Any particular places where we went off-track (too much problem solving, too analytical, not attentive to the spirit?)
- How did each person feel about the meeting?

Instructions for This Week's Prayer

Your main job during this retreat is not finish this booklet, not "feel" God, but to discover the presence of God within yourself. Take your time. Don't rush through your prayer. Here's how.

Reflect on the fact that God sees you and rest in being beheld. You might tell God something like, "God, you know what I'm thinking and feeling. You know me. You, oh God, behold me right here, right now." Then sit with that thought for a while.

You can only do this if you let yourself slow down and relax. Don't rush. Take the time to appreciate God's care for you.

- Follow the 5 P's (page 12 & 13) each day as you begin.
- At the end of your prayer, write in the pages provided what happened in your prayer.
- Spend time each day filling out this week's assignment in your faith autobiography booklet. Make sure the pages for this week are complete by the next group meeting.

Remember, these are *Exercises*, not a class. You can always repeat a scripture instead of moving to the next one. Don't worry about finishing the booklet, or about un-prayed scripture. That's not the point of the Exercises.

We urge you to repeat any scripture that continues to speak to you. Do so until you feel it is "done."

Week 3, Day 1

Luke 4:16-30 - Jesus walks right through the Nazarenes. He wants to bring everyone to Him, even me.

I begin by imagining God gazing at me all the time, regarding me tenderly with great love. As you come to the end of your prayer time, try to make your prayer a dialog. You might talk with your Creator, or with Jesus, or with the Spirit.

After your prayer time, please write your journal entry here:

Week 3, Day 2

Begin by imagining God gazing at you all the time, regarding you tenderly and with great love.

Prayer of Consideration

When they think of creation, many people focus on time such as the days from Genesis, or the birth of a child. But I want to stop and consider that if God is unchanging, then God creative force never ends. What if God creates all things at every moment, out of nothing? How does it affect me to think about creation this way?

God chose my birth place and date, my parents, my attributes; God chose everything about me. God's passionate love burns at my core and continues to shape me now and always.

The Bible says that a fully-alive person reveals the glory of God. So if I become the person God intended, I'll show God's glory. Do I want to become fully alive, to reveal God's glory? I am intelligent and free. I believe I can learn to do this.

I, like all creatures, have a purpose. My unique talents and traits support that purpose. I can express God's hope in me if I discover that purpose and to live it out. Do I want to?

God gives me free will. This means I can choose to follow my purpose or not. It makes sense then, that I should use and enjoy certain things and not others, depending on whether they help me live out my purpose. Following God's will creates love. This is what God hopes for all of us.

What are my thoughts and feelings on this? How does praying about this affect me?

As I come to the end of prayer today, I talk over my prayer time with God - how it was for me. Then I write what happened in prayer today.

Week 3, Day 3

Begin by imagining God gazing at you always, regarding you tenderly.

Psalm 103 - Although life is short, Yahweh forgives, protects, and guides me. Bless Yahweh my soul!

Near the end of your prayer, talk to God the Father, the Son, and/or Spirit, or anyone present in your prayer. Write your experiences and thoughts here:

Week 3, Day 4

When you turn toward God in prayer, begin by noting how tenderly God gazes on you.

Hosea 11:1-4 - As God did for Israel, God protected me in my childhood. In what ways does God still guard me?

Near the end of your prayer, dialog with God. Talk to the Father, Son, and/or the Spirit, or anyone present in your prayer. Then write your journal entry here:

Week 3, Day 5

When you turn toward God in prayer, begin by noting how lovingly God gazes on you.

Job 1:21; & Chapters 38, 40:1-5 - "Who is this obscuring my designs with his empty-headed words?" When do I obscure God's design?

Read slowly, stop and consider words and phrases that touch you; speak with God about them. There's no need to finish all the passages.

Near the end of your prayer, talk to the Father, Son, Spirit. Afterwards, please write your journal entry here:

_____

_____

_____

_____

_____

_____

_____

_____

_____

_____

_____

Week 3, Day 6

When you turn toward God in prayer, begin by noting how God gazes at you, how tenderly and powerfully God regards you.

Isaiah 45:7-13 - Like the potter forming a pot, God creates me and determines my use.

Near the end of your prayer time, dialog with God. Talk to the Father, Son, or Spirit. Afterwards, please write.

_____

_____

_____

_____

_____

_____

_____

_____

_____

_____

_____

Week 3, Day 7

When you turn toward God, begin by noting how lovingly God gazes at you.

Luke 4:16-30 Jesus reads from Isaiah to show who he is.

Go back and read what you wrote on page 44-45, then repeat this passage. This time, focus on ideas, desires, or feelings that were particularly strong, places where you felt great encouragement, love for God, or joy – like refreshing waterfalls. Also, pray about thoughts or feelings that seemed especially hard, confusing, or disturbing, any places you felt discouraged or angry, or places where you felt nothing at all, the sorrow. Near the end of your prayer time, dialog with God the Father, Son, Spirit, or others present in your prayer (such as Mary or an apostle). Afterwards, please write:

WEEK 4

At today's meeting, you will hear about Ignatius' Principle and Foundation, which says:

I am created to praise, reverence, and serve God our Lord, and by this means, to save my soul. The other things on the face of the earth are created to help me attain the end for which I am created.

Hence, I should make use of them as far as they help me in the attainment of my end, and must rid myself of them if they prove a hindrance to me.

Therefore, I must make myself indifferent to all created things, as far as I am allowed by free choice and are not under any prohibition. As far as I am concerned, I should not prefer health to sickness, riches to poverty honor to dishonor a long life to a short life. The same holds true for all other things.

My one desire and choice should be what is more conducive to the end for which I am created.

Our meeting will consist of these parts:

- Opening prayer (page 6)
- Guided Meditation
- Individual prayer
- Group spiritual direction
- Large group discussion
- Closing prayer (page 7)

Questions for Today's Prayer

- How does my own spiritual foundation compare to the one Ignatius proposed in his Principle and Foundation?
- Do I feel that my spiritual foundation is adequate? Why or why not? What would make it better?
- Name some of the values that I hold that influence my choices.

Group Spiritual Direction Instructions

The purpose of Group Spiritual Direction is to keep our focus on what God is doing.

- Please don't solve other's problems.
- Please don't give advice.
- Keep the focus on the person who is sharing.

Speak
Each person in the group is invited to share his or her reflection. You don't have to share, but remember, this is how group spiritual direction works—people sharing their faith lives with others. It gives Spirit an opportunity to be active . As you share, address these questions:

- How did the reading affect me as I prayed?
- What was my experience?
- During my prayer, one of the main feelings I had was _____.
- Where was God in this experience for me?

Listen
Listeners are asked to focus on the speaker. Listen for God in what the person is sharing. What is God saying to that person? What is God saying to you as you listen? After a person has shared, the facilitator will invite you all to share your response to what you have <u>heard</u>.

- Share what you feel God is saying to that person.
- Share what you feel God is saying to you.

Review
At the end of the sharing session, once everyone has shared, take some time to evaluate the process.
- How well did we stay focused on each speaker?
- Any particular places where we went off-track (too much problem solving, too analytical, not attentive to the spirit?)
- How did each person feel about the meeting?

Instructions for This Week's Prayer

Your main job during this retreat is not finish this booklet, not "feel" God, but to discover the presence of God within yourself.

Take your time. Don't rush through your prayer. Here are some tips.

Reflect on the fact that God sees you and rest in being beheld. You might tell God something like, "God, you know what I'm thinking and feeling. You know me. You, oh God, behold me right here, right now." Then sit with that thought for a while. You can only do this if you let yourself slow down and relax.

- Don't rush. Take the time to appreciate God's care for you.
- Follow the 5 P's and C (page 12 & 13) each day as you begin.
- At the end of your prayer, write in the pages provided what happened in your prayer.

Spend time each day filling out this week's assignment in your faith autobiography booklet. Make sure the pages for this week are complete by the next group meeting.

Remember, these are *Exercises*, not a class. You can always repeat a scripture instead of moving to the next one. Don't worry about finishing the booklet, or about un-prayed scripture. That's not the point of the Exercises. The point is to grow closer to God.

We urge you to repeat on another day any scripture that continues to speak to you. Do so on following days until you feel it is "done."

Week 4, Day 1

Ephesians 1: 3-14 God chose me as one who believes in, trusts, and loves Him.

While writing His hopes for me, God has written on my heart a deep desire to fulfill those hopes. What a gift! I want to discover what those hopes and desires are, so from now on, I'll ask God for what I want in prayer. Today, I ask for the grace to know more deeply how much God loves me.

Also, I'll start to think about how seriously I take the Exercises, and whether or not I want to continue with a deeper commitment for the next seven months. Where do I feel called? Can I commit to an hour of prayer a day until May? Along with my other material, I pray about this decision for the next few days.

Near the end of your prayer time, dialog with God or anyone present in your prayer. Afterwards, please write your journal entry here:

Week 4, Day 2

2 Corinthians 5:14-18 – God has chosen not to let sin destroy creation so I share in Jesus' risen life.

While writing His hopes for me, God has written on my heart a deep desire to fulfill those hopes. What a gift! I want to discover what those hopes and desires are, so from now on, I'll ask God for what I want in prayer. Today, I ask for the grace to know more deeply how much God loves me.

I also consider how seriously I take the Exercises, and whether or not I want to continue with a deeper commitment for the next seven months. Where do I feel called? Can I commit to an hour of prayer a day until May?

Near the end of my time, I'll dialog with God (triple colloquy). Afterwards, as usual, I write my journal entry here:

_____

_____

_____

_____

_____

_____

_____

_____

Week 4, Day 3

Romans 8:14-17, 26-27 - Everyone moved by the Spirit is a child of God, so as a son or daughter, I will inherit life with Jesus.

Today, I ask for the grace to know more deeply how much God loves me. I also consider how seriously I take the Exercises, and whether or not I want to continue with a deeper commitment for the next seven months. Where do I feel called? Can I commit to an hour of prayer a day until May?

Near the end of your prayer time, dialog with God (colloquy). Talk to the Father, Son, and/or Spirit. Afterwards, please write your journal entry here:

Week 4, Day 4

Luke 15: 11-32 - The Prodigal's father loved his children like God loves me.

Almighty and ever-caring God, thank you for putting your love in my heart. Today, I ask for the grace to know more deeply how much you love me. I praise and thank you through Jesus Christ our Lord. Amen. I also consider how seriously I take the Exercises, and whether or not I want to continue with a deeper commitment for the next seven months. Where do I feel called? Can I commit to an hour of prayer a day until May?

Near the end of your prayer time, perform a colloquy. Talk to the Father, Son, and/or Spirit. Afterwards, please write your journal entry here:

Week 4, day 5

Luke 13:10-17 - Jesus doesn't let custom or rules hinder God's healing gift. He wants to heal every person who suffers.

Almighty and ever-caring God, thank you for establishing your love in my heart. Today, I ask for the grace to know more deeply how much you love me. I praise and thank you through Jesus Christ our Lord. Amen. I also consider how seriously I take the Exercises, and whether or not I want to continue with a deeper commitment for the next seven months. Where do I feel called? Can I commit to an hour of prayer a day until May?

Near the end of your prayer time, practice colloquy with God. After your prayer time, please write your journal entry here:

Week 4, Day 6

Repeat Prayer of Consideration:

- Read through page 46 again as well as what you wrote that day. Ask God what you should learn this time.
- Sit quietly and allow God to speak again.
- Notice any ideas, desires, feelings that were particularly strong and good, (joys) and those that seem to be especially hard or confusing or disturbing (sorrows).
- Go back to any sorrow. Ask God about the emotions you are experiencing. Sit and listen carefully.
- Return to your joys. Again, ask God for enlightenment. What about these places energized and lightened you? What refreshed you?
- Near the end of your prayer time, practice colloquy (talking things over) with God. You might talk with your Creator, or with Jesus of Nazareth, or the Holy Spirit.
- After your prayer time, please write your journal entry here:

_____

_____

_____

_____

_____

_____

_____

Week 4, Day 7

Repeat one of the scripture passages from this week – your choice.

- Read and pray through the scripture you've chosen. Ask God what you should learn this time.
- Reread what you wrote last time you prayed with this scripture. Sit quietly then, and allow God to speak again.
- Notice any ideas, desires, feelings that were particularly strong and good, and those that seem to be especially hard or confusing or disturbing.
- Return to the places you felt discouragement, revulsion, anger, or even nothing at all: those deep, dark sorrows. Ask God to talk to you about the emotions you are experiencing. Sit and listen carefully.
- Also, return to the joys. Ask God for enlightenment. What about these places energized and lightened you? What refreshed you?

At our next group meeting, I will be asked if I'll continue in the Spiritual Exercises in Everyday Life or not. I consider again how seriously I take the Spiritual Exercises. Do I want to continue with a deeper commitment? Do I have the time? Do I have the resolve? Where do I feel called? Can I commit to an hour of prayer a day until May? If I choose to continue, here's what I'll agree to:

- Submit my completed Faith Autobiography booklet or a typed faith autobiography paper
- Commit to daily prayer – usually an hour
- Attend seven monthly meetings (November through May)
- Meet with my assigned director on my own time, starting in October (weekly or bi-weekly according to schedule)
- Keep my prayer journal
- Pay any fee for the retreat

Near the end of your prayer time, practice colloquy (talking things over with God), then write your journal entry here:

WEEK 5

Today's meeting focuses on the end of the Preparation Days and moving into the Spiritual Exercises.

The meeting will consist of these aspects:

- Opening prayer (page 6)
- Presentation
- Personal prayer using questions in the next page
- Group spiritual direction
- Closing prayer (page 7)

Questions for Prayer

- What gifts have I received from the Preparation Days Retreat?
- What are some of the misgivings I have about committing to the full Retreat?
- Which of those are from God? Which are from myself?
- Where do I believe God is calling me right now?

Group Spiritual Direction Questions

Use the questions above or the material you prayed about this week for your sharing. The purpose of Group Spiritual Direction is to keep our focus on what God is doing

- No problem solving
- No advice giving
- Keep the focus on the person who is sharing

Group Spiritual Direction Instructions

As usual, we'll follow the instructions for group spiritual direction during our group time.

Share

You don't have to share, but sharing gives the Spirit an opportunity to be active within the group process. This is how group spiritual direction works. We invite you to share your experience. As you share, address these issues:

- Share how the reading affected you as you prayed
- Share your experience
- Share a feeling
- Share where God was in this experience

Listen

When a person is speaking, we as listeners are asked to focus on the one speaking. Listen for God in what the person is sharing. What is God saying to that person? What is God saying to you as you listen?

- After a person has shared, the facilitator will invite you all to share your response to what you have heard
- Share what you feel God is saying to that person
- Share what you feel God is saying to you

Review

- At the end of the sharing session, once everyone has shared, take some time to evaluate the process.
- How well did we stay focused on each speaker?
- Any special places where we were off track (too much problem solving, too analytical, not attentive to the spirit)?
- How did each person feel about the meeting?

Review of Prayer

From now on, practice this Review of Prayer after every prayer session.

Imagine that you're alone after a long visit with a good friend. You can recall how you talked about all sorts of things: politics, family, and other friends.

So now, recall words you said or heard, and identify feelings you had during different parts of the conversation. You may have settled some things, but you know there are still unresolved or unfinished issues, too.

You can probably name the general feeling of your time together – good, wonderful, painful, boring, etc. When you make a review of prayer, you do much the same thing only with the conversation between you and God.

Look back over your prayer time to evaluate what you experienced. You don't need to repeat the experience. Just notice things about it: how you began, and the major ideas, your emotions.

- Note movements that were very strong – the joys and sorrows, and evaluate them. Were those feelings peaceful, disturbing, fearful?
- How did you feel towards God?
- Did your prayer increase or decrease your faith or assurance in your choices?
- Write what you discover in your journal.

Instructions for this Week's Prayer

- Pray each day following 5 P's and C (pages 12 and 13).
- Pray through the material given for each day.
- Write in the pages provided what happened in your prayer.

Remember, these are *Exercises*, not a class. You can always repeat a scripture instead of moving to the next one. Do this as long as it continues to speak to you.

Ignatius' Principle and Foundation

Each person is created to praise and revere God and live according to God's will. This is the original purpose of each human life. Whoever praises and reverences God will reach heaven.

All things on earth are meant to help a person come to his or her original purpose. The only thing that makes sense, then, is that you use whatever helps you understand and live out your original purpose, and reject everything that separates you from your original purpose. When you're under no obligation in conscience, you ought to keep yourself free of any fixed preference or attachment for any specific created thing.

This means that before you make a decision, you don't determine ahead of time what you can't live without. For example, you shouldn't do everything to keep yourself healthy even though you know that exposing yourself to illness would help someone else. Or you'll do everything to become richer, or you'll do nothing to diminish your importance, or your notoriety. Nor should you choose just to ensure longevity.

Instead, when choices arise, you should choose first to follow Christ, wherever that takes you. If you do this, poverty, wealth, sickness, health, notoriety, long life, short life all become consequences of your decision, not the actual choice itself. And you'll keep balanced before created things. To set yourself to live in careful balance, choose only what leads more directly and more certainly to your original purpose, and thus more certainly toward God's will.

Week 5, Day 1

Ephesians 2:1-10 - My whole life is God's work of art. God chose to create me.

I ask for the grace to know how much God loves me.

Whisper or read the passage aloud. Then close the Bible and recall words and phrases. Let each word fill you. Listen and talk to God. God gives gifts and limitations that help define choices and desires. My task is to find what God hopes and wants for me. I do this by discovering my deepest desires.

After you have finished reciting the Our Father at the end of your prayer time, take a brief time for another exercise: Review of Prayer, page 78.

Week 5, Day 2
Discernment

The world is a full of stuff. I'm attracted to some, repelled by others, indifferent to most. Sometimes I know which are important for me—I need love and food to survive, for example.

Mostly, I'm free to choose. But I know from experience that some things make me more loving towards God and other people, while other things make me more selfish and less loving, even towards myself. But decisions can be difficult. I don't always know which choice is right for me, which bring me to God. And lots of times I just want what I want.

The truth is, I can't assume any particular thing—riches or poverty, health or sickness, notoriety or obscurity, etc. —is right for me. None of these automatically take me to God.

And I'm attracted to things, especially stuff that doesn't lead me to God. So now I want to change that. I want to learn how to choose what leads me to God and my truest self. This means I don't automatically assume something is good for me. Instead, I'll choose whatever leads me to greater love for God and others.

Maybe this seems obvious and simple, but it can be challenging. Attachment to good things and opportunities can cause me to act against my truest self. If I have an attachment to being rich, for instance, I might choose to compromise my values to make more money instead of following Christ. I know I'm capable of wrecking my own life by trying to force God to agree with my poor choices. I know I can hurt others if I fail to live true to myself and to what God wants for me.

I need God to help me choose things and actions that will move me toward my best self. I can't do it on my own. I trust that God knows which alternative is right for me, and I trust God will tell me what and when I need to know, and I thank God for that insight. Amen.

After you have finished reciting the Our Father at the end of your prayer time, take a brief time for another exercise: Review of Prayer. Then write your prayer experience here.

Week 5, Day 3

Genesis 22:1-19 – This person was willing to give up the most precious thing in his life because God asked.

I ask for the grace to know how much God loves me.

After you have finished reciting the Our Father at the end of your prayer time, take a brief time for another exercise: Review of Prayer (page 78).

_____

_____

_____

_____

_____

_____

_____

_____

_____

_____

_____

Week 5, Day 4

Repetition:

When I begin, I ask for the grace to know how much God loves me.

I look back over my week. I choose a prayer time where something sad or ugly, or very little occurred, and/or a joy where I found love of God and light and insight. I pray again with that scripture. I recite the Our Father after my prayer time. Then, I take a brief time for Review of Prayer (page 78).

Week 5, Day 5

Isaiah 6: 1-13 - Isaiah is called by the Lord; so am I. Am I ready to respond?

I ask for the grace to know how much God loves me. After you have finished reciting the Our Father at the end of your prayer time, do a Review of Prayer.

Week 5, Day 6

Romans 8:28-39 - The Lord calls me and shapes all things toward my good.

Though I can't grow toward God on my own, no power compares to God's. I ask for the grace to know how much God loves me. After I have finished reciting the Our Father at the end of my prayer time, I review my prayer.

Week 5, Day 7

I ask for the grace to know how much God loves me.

Repetition: I look back on the sorrows and joys and /or pray with the following prayer:

Almighty God, no living creature can make itself come to be all by itself. You create all things and bring them back to yourself. And nothing in me can force You to love me or want me to be alive. Since before I was conceived, you have loved me with an everlasting love. Now Your love burns free and never-ending, at the core of me. I acknowledge You alone as Lord, living and reigning forever and ever. Amen.

After you have finished reciting the Our Father at the end of your prayer time, do a Review of Prayer.

The Examen

At the end of every day, take ten minutes to examine your day. It should go something like this:

Thank You

Everything is a gift from You, God, my Creator. I give you thanks and praise for the gifts of the day.

Help Me

Holy Spirit, give me increased awareness of how you are guiding my life.

I Love You

Jesus, you are present in my life today. Together, let's look t at my day. Let me see through your loving eyes. When did I listen to your voice today? When did I resist listening to you today?

I'm Sorry

I ask for healing for ...

I ask your forgiveness for ...

Be With Me

Filled with hope and a firm belief in your love I entrust myself in your care. Continue to be with me each day.

Amen.

WEEK 6

There is no group meeting this week. The formal Preparation Days Retreat is finished. However, if you are continuing into the Spiritual Exercises, please pray through this material before going on, unless your director tells you otherwise.

Instructions for This Week's Prayer

- Prepare again for the next day (choose scripture, grace, etc.)
- Pray each day following the methods you've been using.
- Pray through the material given for each day.
- Write in the pages provided what happened in your prayer.
- In the evening, choose a passage and grace for tomorrow's prayer.
- Read through the passage if possible.

You can use this structure every day after the retreat is over, or if you are continuing on to the Exercises.

Remember, you can always repeat a scripture instead of moving to the next one. Repeat a scripture as long as it continues to speak to you.

Week 6, Day 1

Romans 7: 14-25 - Paul knew he was prone to sin, just as I am. But Jesus has defeated that evil.

After you have finished reciting the Our Father at the end of your prayer time, take a brief time for another exercise: Review of Prayer.

_____

_____

_____

_____

_____

_____

_____

_____

_____

_____

_____

_____

_____

Week 6, Day 2

Repetition: Read through the Principle and Foundation every day this week. (Page 79) Today, use it for prayer.

Sometimes these exercises will console me; other times they seem desolate. When these swings happen, if I pay attention, and accept them patiently, I'll learn a lot about God, myself, and prayer.

After you have finished reciting the Our Father at the end of your prayer time, take a brief time for another exercise: Review of Prayer.

Week 6, Day 3

Hebrews 2: 5-13 - Jesus is my brother and is with me all the time, even though I don't always recognize Him. What does God see in me?

After you've finished reciting the Our Father at the end of your prayer time, take time for another exercise: Review of Prayer.

Week 6, Day 4

Repetition: I choose a scripture that touched me and repeat it.

After you have finished reciting the Our Father at the end of your prayer time, take a brief time for another exercise: Review of Prayer.

Week 6, Day 5

John 1: 1-8 - Through Jesus all things came to be. I can rest in Him who is "the Beginning."

After you have finished reciting the Our Father at the end of your prayer time, take a brief time for another exercise: Review of Prayer.

Week 6, Day 6

Deuteronomy 30: 15-20 - God respects me so much that I've been given the ability to choose life or death in every situation. All those who have gone before me have had the same choice.

After you have finished reciting the Our Father at the end of your prayer time, take a brief time for another exercise: Review of Prayer.

Week 6 Day 7

Look back on the joys and sorrows of the past six weeks. Choose one to pray with again.

After you have finished reciting the Our Father at the end of your prayer time, take a brief time for another exercise: Review of Prayer.

Thank you!

Thank-you for participating in the Preparation Days Retreat. We hope it has enriched your life. Sharing in your faith life and providing the retreat for you have touched us deeply and it's been a pleasure serving you.

If you are continuing with the Exercises, we welcome you. Your director will be getting in touch with you soon.

Our first meeting will be:

_____

We love you!

Your Retreat Team